LIBRARIANS

BY JODY JENSEN SHAFFER

Wonder Books

An Imprint of The Child's World®

childsworld.com

The Child's World®
childsworld.com

Published by The Child's World®
800-599-READ • www.childsworld.com

Photography Credits
wavebreakmedia/Shutterstock.com, cover, 4, 5, 6, 16, 21;
Tyler Olson/Shutterstock.com, 7, 12; Jody Jensen Shaffer,
8, 9; Rob Marmion/Shutterstock.com, 11; Bruce VanLoon/
Shutterstock.com, 13; Drazen Zigic/Shutterstock.com,
14; FREEPIK2/Shutterstock.com, 15; US National Park
Service, 17; Andy Dean Photography/Shutterstock.com, 18;
GaudiLab/Shutterstock.com, 19; LanKS/Shutterstock.com,
22; Mega Pixel/Shutterstock.com, 23

ISBN Information
9781503858329 (Reinforced Library Binding)
9781503860001 (Portable Document Format)
9781503861367 (Online Multi-user eBook)
9781503862722 (Electronic Publication)

LCCN 2021952631

Printed in the United States of America

ABOUT THE AUTHOR

Jody Jensen Shaffer is an award-winning poet and the author of more than 80 books of fiction and nonfiction for children. She lives in Missouri with her family.

CONTENTS

Hello! My Name Is Ruben 4

I Could Be a Librarian! 5

Learn About This Neighborhood Helper! 6

Who Can Become a Librarian? 7

Meet a Librarian! 8

Where Can I Learn to Be a Librarian? 10

What Does a Librarian Need to Do the Job? 12

Where Does a Librarian Work? 14

Who Works with Librarians? 16

When Is an Orca in a Library? 17

I Want to Be a Librarian! 18

Why Don't You Try Being a Librarian? 20

Glossary. 22

Think About It. 23

Find Out More. 24

Index. 24

Hello! My Name Is Ruben.

Many people live and work in my neighborhood. Each of them helps the neighborhood in different ways.

I thought of all the things I like to do. I like to read books. I like to learn new things. I like to help people. How could I help my neighborhood when I grow up?

I Could Be a Librarian!

Librarians like to read books. Books teach us about the world. Librarians like to help people. Librarians help others learn about the world, too!

If you love books, you could be a librarian when you grow up.

Learn About This Neighborhood Helper!

The best way to learn is to ask questions. Words such as *who, what, where, when*, and *why* will help me learn about being a librarian.

Where Can I Learn More?

American Library Association (ALA): www.ala.org

American Association of School Librarians: www.ala.org/aasl

Asking a librarian questions will help you learn more about the job.

Who Can Become a Librarian?

Children who like to read may want to be librarians. They must enjoy helping others. Librarians help people find information. They help people find books.

They teach people to use computers. Librarians are important neighborhood helpers. They lead story times for children. They put on programs for adults. Some librarians work in schools. Some work in **government**.

How Can I Explore This Job?

Visit your local library. Talk to a librarian about the job. Offer to help shelve books. Maybe you could help with story time. Ask a librarian what they like best about the job and which parts of the job are challenging.

Meet a Librarian!

This is Katie. She is the Branch **Manager** at a library in Missouri. It is a public library. Anyone can use it. Katie is a librarian, too. She helps people find books. She helps them use computers. She also leads other librarians and library workers.

Librarians work in public libraries, schools, and other organizations.

Katie loved to read as a child. Her family had many books in their home. Katie was shy around people. She spent a lot of time reading. Katie likes to do things with her family when she is not working. They like to read, too.

Librarians are organized and work well with others. They assign **call numbers** to books. Once a book has a call number, it can be easily found in the library's **catalog**. A librarian may need to do minor repairs on books that have been damaged, too.

How Many Librarians Are There?
About 143,500 people work as librarians in the United States.

Where Can I Learn to Be a Librarian?

Katie went to college for six years to become a librarian. She has a master's degree in library science. She learned how libraries work. She learned how computers organize books. She learned all the ways libraries help people.

How Much School Will I Need?

Most librarians have a master's degree in library science (MLS). School librarians may also need a teaching certificate, depending on their state's requirements.

Librarians are good at researching and helping people find the information they need.

What Does a Librarian Need to Do the Job?

What Are Some Tools I Will Use?
- Books
- Book scanners
- Carts
- Computers

Katie needs a computer to do her job. She uses it to find books. She uses it to help people with the Internet. She uses it to **schedule** employees. She also uses it to plan programs. Katie also needs books to do her job! Books take a lot of space. Katie needs space for the books. She needs room for programs. She needs tables and chairs, too.

Katie uses special words to talk about her job. She calls the books a **collection**. Most libraries have collections for kids and for adults. Katie calls library visitors **patrons**. Katie uses the word *privacy*. She doesn't share what someone has asked her.

What Clothes Will I Wear?

- Business clothes
- Comfortable shoes
- Name tag/ID

Where Does a Librarian Work?

Katie works in a public library. It is near a big city.

She gets to work early in the morning. She and her staff turn on the computers. They **display** books for people to borrow. They gather books patrons put on hold. They prepare rooms for programs.

What's It Like Where I'll Work?

Librarians work indoors. They often work in big buildings. It is usually quiet in a library. Libraries can be noisy during story times for children.

Finding a book on a library shelf is easy if you know its call number.

Who Works with Librarians?

Many people help Katie do her job. Katie works with other librarians. She works with front desk staff. They help patrons find books. They help with the computers. They organize programs. It takes a team of people to make a good library!

Library staff members lead weekly story times for their young patrons.

16

When Is an Orca in a Library?

When the body of an orca was found in Glacier Bay National Park and Preserve in Alaska, park service workers thought it could be a great educational opportunity for the community. After scientists studied how the whale died, all the bones of the skeleton were cleaned and preserved. Then the bones were put back together.

The community decided to display the skeleton in the public library. The orca measures 12 feet (3.6 meters) long and hangs above the children's reading room. What a cool view!

I Want to Be a Librarian!

I think being a librarian would be a great way to

be a neighborhood helper. I am organized and work well with others. I love books and reading. Someday I may help you find a book!

How Might My Job Change?
Librarians will use computers more and more. Librarians may help patrons with things they need. They may help them find a doctor. They may help them find homes. Libraries may become community centers.

Some librarians work in medical and law libraries. They research and analyze documents and journals.

Why Don't You Try Being a Librarian?

Do you think you would like to be a librarian? A librarian knows that reading is an important skill for the job. You can get better by reading every day. Pick books you enjoy. Pick books that challenge you. Read all kinds of books. You could even start a book club! Your friends can read the same book. Meet and talk about it. Tell what you liked and what you didn't like. Take a trip to your library. Take a tour. Find out everything a library can do for you.

I Didn't Know That!

Carla Hayden is a librarian. She is the Librarian of Congress. She works in Washington, DC. The Library of Congress is the biggest library in the world. Hayden is the first woman to lead the library. She is the first African American to do so, too. She began her career in Chicago. She was a children's librarian. Then she taught college library classes. She also led a public library in Maryland. Hayden earned her PhD from the University of Chicago.

Maybe one day I will be a librarian!

Glossary

call numbers (KOL NUHM-burz): A unique combination of numbers and letters that tells where a book belongs in a library.

catalog (KA-tuh-log): A list of all the books, magazines, movies, and newspapers in a library.

certificate (sur-TIF-ih-kut): An official document saying someone may do a certain job.

collection (kuh-LEK-shun): A group of similar things.

display (dih-SPLAY): An arrangement of things.

government (GUH-vurn-ment): The group of people who control and make decisions for a country or state.

manager (MAN-ih-juhr): A person who leads people.

papyrus (pah-PY-ruhs): A plant people used to write on.

patrons (PAY-truns): People who use the services of a library.

schedule (SKEDJ-yoo-ull): A plan of things to do and the times to do them.

Think About It

- Do you want to be a librarian when you grow up? Why or why not? What personality traits make a good librarian? What would be the most challenging part of the job?

- Librarians must be very good at fact-checking and knowing what a reliable resource looks like. Do you agree or disagree with this statement? Explain your reasoning.

- Imagine that you are a librarian. A young patron needs help finding information for a report. How would you help? What's the first thing you'd tell your patron about researching a topic?

- Public libraries are an important part of the community. In addition to providing reading materials, libraries are used to hold club meetings and classes. Some libraries are used as voting centers, too. Do you attend your public library for a special program? Is there a class or event you wish your library offered?

Find Out More

IN THE LIBRARY

Dennis, Elizabeth, and Natalie Kwee (illustrator). *If You Love Books, You Could Be . . . .* New York, NY: Simon Spotlight, 2020.

Honders, Christine. *Why Should I Listen to My Librarian?* New York, NY: Rosen, 2020.

Waxman, Laura Hamilton. *Librarian Tools*. Minneapolis, MN: Lerner, 2020.

ON THE WEB

Visit our website for links about librarians:

childsworld.com/links

Note to Parents, Caregivers, Teachers, and Librarians: We routinely verify our Web links to make sure they are safe and active sites. So encourage your readers to check them out!

Index

book club, 20

call numbers, 9
carts, 12
catalog, 9
certificate, teaching, 10
collection, 13
college, 10, 20

display, 14, 17

Hayden, Carla, 20
holds, book, 14

library assistants, 16
Library of Congress, 20
library science, 10
library technicians, 16

manager, 8
money, 14

orca, 17

papyrus, 5

patrons, 13, 14, 16, 19
privacy, 13
public library, 8, 14, 17, 20

reading, 9, 17, 18, 20
repairs, book, 9

scanners, 12
schedule, 12
schools, 7, 10
shoes, comfortable, 13
story time, 7, 15